Learning from
THE QUR'AN
with
AHMED & AISHA

UMM HAIDER ALI

iman imprints

Copyright © 2024, Umm Haider Ali

All rights reserved.

No part of this publication may be reproduced, distributed, or transmitted in any form or by any means, including photocopying, recording, or other electronic or mechanical methods, without the prior written permission of the publisher.

Book Cover by Faisal Iqbal
Illustrations by Faisal Iqbal

Table of Contents

Iqra' - Read 01

Al-Qalam - The Pen 14

The Fruits of Jannah 24

The Sun or The Moon, which is Greater? 37

Time 47

Learning from the Qur'an
with Ahmed and Aisha

Iqra'
Read

The Habitat

It was a warm, sunny day and Ahmed was sitting at his desk at home, trying to study. He was studying for a school project he had to complete later that day with his best friend, Bilal. But Ahmed was bored. He didn't feel like reading anything. He looked outside of the window, thinking how much better it would be at the park.

Ever since the start of the summer holidays, Ahmed would often be found at his local park, enjoying the secret little hideout he called, "The Habitat." There, he had made a whole load of new friends who would drop by for a visit. These friends were different though. Some had two legs, some had four and some had none.

Can you guess what type of friends he may have?

Not wanting to sit at home any longer, Ahmed stood up and headed for the park.

Ahmed loves nature

At the park, neatly tucked away behind some trees and bushes was The Habitat. It was a perfect, quiet spot where Ahmed built little homes for his animal friends. He built a worm compost by digging a small hole and layering it with leaves and damp soil. He loved watching how the worms moved and wriggled their way slowly in and out of their homes. He made a small den out of leaves, sticks, and stones for all the creepy crawlies to stay in. He also placed an old clay bowl on the ground and used it as a bird bath. Watching the different types of animals come out or fly down to eat and drink was amazing. On warmer days, Ahmed would take some water to fill up the bird bath, as well as some leftover scraps of food like bread, seeds, and nuts, and would spread them around The Habitat. Ahmed would also place some on an old tree stump and then hide behind a bush and watch the birds and squirrels come out for their meal.

One day, Ahmed laid out the food on the tree stump and was about to get up and hide, but to his surprise, a bird he had not seen before, had flown down and started pecking at the food. The bird had a bright red face and yellow feathers - it was a fantastic sight! 'Wow! This is amazing!' he thought. 'It's not even afraid of me being here.' He felt so proud! The bird was chirping happily, and Ahmed's smile grew wider, but he was afraid to move as he didn't want to disturb the bird. As he stood statue-still watching the red-faced bird, he didn't notice that the rest of the food he had placed around the trees was all being taken too!

'What! I stood there, right in the middle where all the birds and squirrels could see me, and they ate all the food without me knowing. Wow! That is BRILLIANT!' - Ahmed laughed to himself and thought how amazing it is to have built a special relationship with the animals - He could now sit among the animals without worrying about scaring them off.

'Whoever is kind to the creatures of God, is kind to himself.' **Hadith Bukhari.**

Ahmed was enjoying his time outside so much that he forgot about the school project he had to complete with Bilal.

Ahmed keeps his promise

"Ahmed, Ahmed!" shouted Bilal, "Where is he?" Bilal was looking for Ahmed at the park and then he remembered where he could be and ran towards The Habitat.

"Sshh!" Ahmed gestured, putting his finger on his lips to keep Bilal quiet. "Oh, the birds have flown away now!" "What are you doing?" asked Bilal.

"I'm busy, watching the animals," replied Ahmed.

"Why? Are they your pets?" laughed Bilal.

"No, well, actually, kind of." Ahmed started thinking to himself.

Bilal looked at him confused.

"I mean, I know who they are and I see them almost every day. They eat the food I give them and aren't afraid when I sit with them." Ahmed said proudly.

"Really! That's so cool!" Bilal said with a big smile on his face.

Bilal and Ahmed had known each other since they were at pre-school, and as they were neighbours they'd done everything together and were best friends. But, for the past few weeks, Bilal had been busy helping his dad at their shop and couldn't see Ahmed as much as he wanted.

"Do you remember we need to hand in our school project? You said you were coming over to mine this afternoon to complete it." Bilal was a little upset as Ahmed never broke his promises.

"Sorry! I got a little carried away watching the animals. I was at home before, trying to study for it, but you know me with books, the words were not coming out, and I couldn't study. I decided to come here, it's just so much nicer being outdoors! Allah's blessed us with all this beautiful nature, Alhumdulilah." Ahmed then laid down with his hands behind his head and looked up at the sky. "Ahmed, we need to do the work, otherwise, we'll get detention! Please, come on." Ahmed sighed and held out his hand for Bilal to pull him up. They both walked back to Bilal's home together.

Ahmed and Bilal learn about the importance of Reading

"Assalamu Alaikum Aunty," said Ahmed.

"Wa Alaikum Salaam, Ahmed, How are you?"

"Alhamdulillah, I am fine – Well, I was until I was reminded, that we have to complete our school project.' Ahmed replied sulkily.

"Ha ha, yes, Bilal told me about the school project. Come sit down and tell me what you have to do," she said with a smile.

Bilal took out his laptop and books from his bag and showed his mum what they were working on.

"The topic is 'Where do things come from?'"

"Oh, Masha Allah, that sounds interesting, I would love to learn more about this with you too."

Ahmed looked at Aunty Maryam with a puzzled face, "Why?" he asked.

"Well, once you learn that Allah is the Creator of everything and how He created it, then you'll also learn about their purpose in the world, Insha'Allah."

"I never looked at it in that way, Subhan' Allah. But does that mean I would have to read?" Ahmed moaned as he slumped back on the chair.

"Yes!" Aunty Maryam patted Ahmed on his shoulders with a smile. "So, boys, what are we finding out about?"

Ahmed looked at the notes "Bread, honey, and oil - where do they come from?"

"Mum buys them from the supermarket," Bilal said jokingly.

Ahmed laughed, but Aunty Maryam had a different way of explaining it and recited an ayah from the Qur'an:

'Bismillaahir–Rahmaanir–Raheem.

And it is He who sends rain from the sky – causing all kinds of plants to grow – producing green stalks from which we bring forth clustered grain. And from palm trees come clusters of dates hanging within reach. There are also gardens of grapevines, olives, and pomegranates, similar in shape but dissimilar in taste. Look at their fruit as it yields and ripens! Indeed, in these are signs for people who believe.'

"And Allah always speaks the truth! That was from Surah Al An'Am, ayah ninety-nine."

Aunty Maryam was a hafidha and Qur'an teacher. Ahmed and Bilal always enjoyed it whenever she recited the Qur'an because she could mention any ayah from the Qur'an and link it to whatever topic was being discussed.

"You see, now that is where you can start from," Aunty Maryam explained.

Ahmed was now happy to do the school project. And with Bilal, they both got started on their work.

They learned that bread comes from wheat grains. They are harvested and then milled into flour before going to the bakers to make the bread. They also learnt how honey is made by bees. They collect nectar from the flowering plants which they take to their hives to make the honey. And for the making of oil, this comes from pressing or squeezing plant seeds at low temperatures. They learnt that there are many types of oils produced by various seeds, like olives, sunflower seeds, and even coconuts. Ahmed and Bilal were very busy writing everything out neatly onto a large poster and printing out and sticking pictures they had found on the internet. They were very pleased with how fast they worked and how much they learnt.

After the boys had completed their project, they could not stop talking about how amazing the creation of Allah is. They spoke about how the things we don't take notice of, could be made into the products we all eat, drink and use every day. Subhan'Allah.

Try look from the Qur'an at the ayahs that talk about wheat, honey, and oil.

Iqra - Read

"Assalamu Alaikum!" Ahmed said as he entered his home.

"Wa Alaikum Salaam, Ahmed," his mother got up from her seat and walked to give Ahmed a big hug. "Go and clean up while I warm your dinner,"

"Oh, I already ate at Aunty Maryam's," replied Ahmed. "Did you manage to finish your project?" Mum asked, then looked at Ahmed's appearance and noticed mud marks on his jeans. "Bilal did come round earlier asking for you, I told him that you were at the park. Looking at the state of your clothes, I'm guessing you went to see the animals again?" Mum said smiling.

"Yeah, it was so cool mama! The animals are all friendly with me now. I love watching them as they come and go, it's amazing where they all come from." And as Ahmed said those last words, he remembered his project and smiled, "Alhumdulilah, Allah truly is Great! I didn't want to do my homework at first. I wanted to stay outside with the animals, but after going to Bilal's house, Aunty Maryam read some verses of the Qur'an, and that taught me that I need to read to learn more."

"Masha Allah Ahmed, that is very good! May Allah

reward Aunty Maryam too, she has helped you to understand how important reading is and helped you in completing your project. Alhumdulilah. Reading is very important. This reminds me of a Surah called Al Alaq, the first Surah to be revealed to our Prophet. Our beloved Prophet Muhammad (SAW) was actually unable to read or write. But he would spend his days and nights in a cave called Hira, to think about and worship the one true God. He didn't want to worship the idols the people of Makkah used to worship, or enjoin in the other bad practices the people used to carry. One day, Angel Jibreel, was sent down by Allah to command Muhamad (SAW) to recite the first five verses of the Qur'an. But Muhammad (SAW) kept saying he couldn't read, and the Angel would squeeze him each time he said this until he was able to recite those verses of Surah Al Alaq. Alhumdulilah, we are gifted with the miracle of the Qur'an so we can read, understand, and practice its teachings like our Prophet did. And do you know from that Surah of Al Alaq, what the first word is?" Mum looked at Ahmed, smiled, and then continued, "To Read!"

Ahmed looked his mum with amazement, "Subhan'Allah. Allah truly is Great."

She then recited the first five ayahs (verses) of the Surah Al-Alaq:-

*"A-oodhu billahi mina- shaytaanir- rajeem
Bismillahir -Rahmanir - Raheem.*

*Read! In the name of your Lord who Created.
He has created man from a clot.
Read! And your Lord is the Most Generous,
Who taught by the pen-
taught humanity what they knew not."*

What can we learn from the story?

Ahmed learned two important lessons that day. The first was that the first word to be revealed to our Prophet Muhammad (SAW) was 'Read.' - Allah (SWT) taught our first Prophet, Adam AS the name of all the things, as He (SWT) has taught our final Messenger Muhammad (SAW) the command to read or recite. The Qur'an was sent as a book of guidance to teach humankind how to live and behave in their everyday lives. – Even though Ahmed did not like reading, he understood its importance. Reading the Qur'an and learning from books, Ahmed is able to appreciate the things around him.

It was narrated that the Prophet (SAW) said: 'Seeking knowledge is a duty upon every Muslim both male and female.' **Hadith ibn Majah.**

The second lesson was Observation. When Ahmed was watching the animals carefully, this helped him to understand and appreciate the living creatures and their environment more. May we continue our love for learning. ***Ameen!***

**Learning from the Qur'an
with Ahmed and Aisha**

Al-Qalam
The Pen

Al Qalam - The Pen

Ahmed and Bilal were sitting in class listening to their teacher, just before the end of school bell rang. The children were asked to complete the second half of their school project with the topic of finding out where things come from.

"I am going to find out where leather comes from for this one," said Bilal, as Bilal and Ahmed walked out of school and headed home.

"Leather? Why did you choose that?" asked Ahmed.

"Well, my Uncle Khalid went to Turkey for his holidays and brought me back a jacket, a cushion cover for my mum, and traditional Turkish slippers for my little brother Omer. And they were all made from leather! I think it's pretty cool how so many things can be made from one material."

"Wow, that is cool!" Ahmed said with a smile.

"Yes! So what are you going to choose?" asked Bilal.

"I don't know yet, I will need to think about it."

"Well don't think too long, I don't want to go looking for you at the park again," laughed Bilal.

Bilal remembered the last time they were doing the project; Ahmed was at the park in his secret hideout watching his animal friends.

"Yeah, yeah, no need to remind me" he replied, feeling a bit embarrassed. "Oh. I know!" said Ahmed excitedly, "I'm going to do it on - Where things come from!"

Bilal scratched his head, looking confused, "Erm, yes that is the topic of project."

"But where do they 'REALLY' come from?" Ahmed looked at Bilal with a big smile.

"Oh, I get it! Masha Allah, that's a clever idea!" Bilal laughed

"Insha Allah, we'll do great on this project too!" said Ahmed.

Ahmed arrived home and heard his Grandma in the sitting room reciting the Qur'an,

"....There is none worthy of worship but Him the Creator of everything. Therefore, worship Him! He is the Guardian of all things."

"Maa!" Ahmed called, "Assalamu Alaikum." Ahmed ran to Grandma to greet her.

"Ahh, Ahmed! Wa Alaikum Salaam." Grandma gave him a big hug and a kiss on his forehead. "How are you, my dear?"

Before Ahmed could reply, his little sister Aisha ran up to him and put her arms around him.

"Ahmed!" Aisha looks up at her brother with a huge grin. "Assalaamu Alaikum Aisha," Ahmed hugged his sister, "Wa Alaikum Salaam," Aisha held on to Ahmed as they went to sit on the sofa.

"Alhamdulillah, I had a good day at school. But Maa, I heard you reciting some verses of the Qur'an. Which Surah were you reading from? You mentioned the word Khaliq. Are you talking about what Allah created?" asked Ahmed.

"Yes, that was from Surah Al An'am, the eighth Surah of the Qur'an.

"Maa was playing farm animals with me and was reciting the Qur'an," said Aisha as she went back onto the floor and played with the animals.

Aisha was four years old. She always enjoyed playing, reading, and talking with Grandma whenever she came over to their house.

"Maa, could you teach me that ayah, please? I am doing a school project on 'where things come from,' and I'd like to use that verse of the Qur'an."

"Of course! Masha Allah, may Allah (SWT) bless you."

Ahmed went to sit down next to her so they could get started on his project.

The Presentation Day

Each child went up to present their topic in front of the class. Interesting subjects were read like; 'Where flowers come from', Where rain comes from'. But Ahmed wanted to answer the question in a different way.

"Ahmed, you're up next," called Miss Higgins, Ahmed's Teacher.

Ahmed walked up to the front of the class and began with the recitation of the Qur'an he had learned with Grandma and then explained them in English. He explained how God, Allah created everything. He spoke about the sun and the planets, the animals, and the plants. He also told them about the first man on earth – Adam - who was taught the names of everything by Allah. After he finished speaking, he smiled and felt very happy with his presentation, but some of the children laughed.

"Quite please children! That was different and interesting Ahmed," said, Miss Higgins. "Well done!" Ahmed returned to his seat feeling a little sad about those who laughed at him. He didn't understand why it was funny.

"Right, who's next? Ah, Bilal! Come up and present your homework please," said Miss Higgins.

Bilal patted Ahmed on his shoulder and smiled to show that he enjoyed Ahmed's presentation. He then went to the front of the class and began to talk about his uncle who went to Turkey and brought some gifts made of leather for his family. He explained that the leather came from the skin of the animals like cows, sheep, and goats. He also spoke about the different uses of leather, like in clothing, bags, and home furnishings, and how they have benefited people for centuries. He then concluded with an ayah of the Quran, Surah Ghafir verse eighty:

"Bismillaahir -Rahmaanir – Raheem. It is God, Allah who provided for you all manner of livestock, that you may ride on some of them and from some, you may derive your food. And other uses in them for them to satisfy your heart desires…"

Some of the children sighed as if they were bored but Bilal smiled and went back to his seat. Just when the teacher was thanking everyone for doing such a great job, the school bell rang and it was time to go home.

Ahmed and Bilal were walking along the corridor on their way out when a group of boys jokingly asked, "So who made Me?" and ran off laughing.

"Don't worry about them, they don't understand." said Bilal, "You spoke the truth, and that's what matters!" Bilal put his arm around Ahmed. Ahmed smiled to thank him, and they carried on walking home.

Allah is with you

"Assalamu Alaikum," said Ahmed, as he entered the house.

"Wa Alaikum Salam," replied Mum "How was school?"

"Okay I guess," replied Ahmed. Before going to wash his hands. he went to sit next to Mum on the sofa, "Mama, what would you do if you know you're saying the truth but people laugh at you?"

"Oh, what happened Ahmed?" asked Mum.

"Well, I was reading out my presentation, and some of the children started to laugh, It really upset me."

Mum brought Ahmed towards her and hugged him.

"Did you know that during the time of our beloved Prophet Muhammad (SAW), the people of Makkah would laugh at him too? They called him names like crazy, a magician and even tried to hurt him! And Allah (SWT) revealed verses of the Qur'an to the Prophet to remind him that Allah is always supporting him. This gave Muhammad (SAW) the strength and confidence to carry out his duty as a Messenger of Allah. We should also do our best to share the knowledge of Islam too, even if it means some people make fun of us.

This reminds me of a Surah called Al Qalam, The Pen."

Ahmed's Mum began to recite the first four verses of the Surah Al Qalam:

*"A-oodhu billahi mina-shaytaanir-rajeem,
Bismillaahir-Rahmaanir-Raheem.*

*Noon. By the Pen and what everyone writes!
By the Grace of your Lord, You, 'o Prophet' are not insane, You will certainly have a never-ending reward, And you are truly a man of outstanding character."*

What can we learn from the story?

Ahmed loves Allah and wanted to share his knowledge with the class, but he learnt that some people may not want to listen and will behave in a manner that can upset him, just like they did with the beloved Prophet Muhammad (SAW). Muhammad (SAW) had full faith in Allah and had the best of manners. If we follow his example, Allah will always support us. May we always have good character, **Ameen!**

**Learning from the Qur'an
with Ahmed and Aisha**

The Fruits of Jannah

The Fruits of Jannah

"He causes the crops to grow for you, and olives and date palms, and grape vines, and all the fruits. Surely in that, here is a sign for a people who ponder." (Surah An Nahl: 11)

It was the school holidays, and Grandma and Grandad had come to visit. Everyone was feeling very warm from the hot weather, which gave Grandma an idea.

"Come on Aisha, I'm taking you out today!" said Grandma.

Aisha started jumping up and down excitedly, "Where are we going?"

"Let's go to the shops and see what we can get to make for a nice cool drink," said Grandma.

"Yeah!" Aisha quickly ran upstairs to get her sunglass and hat. "How do I look? she said with a huge grin.

"Beautiful," Grandma kissed Aisha on the head and went to get her bag but saw Ahmed helping out in the kitchen.

"Ahmed, do you want to come with us to the shops?"

"No, thank you. Hasan, from Palestine, and Bilal will be coming over soon, and their families will join us later for dinner, Insha'Allah. I will stay and help Mum," said Ahmed.

"Oh, that is very kind of you Ahmed, may Allah reward you. Insha'Allah, it will be a lovely gathering. Insha'Allah we will see you all later." Grandma and Aisha gave their salaams and left for the shops.

Surah At Teen

"So, Aisha, tell me about school?" Grandma was holding Aisha's hand as they were walking along the street.

"Alhumdulilah, its good! In madrasah, we were learning about fruits Allah talks about in the Qur'an. I know their Arabic names, there's Teen, Ruman, Talh, Zaytoon, Thamr, and Anab. They are the fruits of Jannah," Aisha said proudly.

"Masha Allah Aisha, that is very good! Do you know what those fruit names are in English?" asked Grandma.

Aisha stopped for a moment to think, "Oh… I don't think I remember, but I may remember when I see them." Aisha smiled nodding her head as they continued walking. "But, I have learnt Surah At-Teen!" and she started to recite the Surah to Grandma.

"A-oodhu billahi mina-shaytaanir-rajeem
"Bismillaahir- Rahmaanir-Raheem,

"By the fig and the olive of Jerusalem,
And Mount Sinai, And this secure city of Makkah,
Indeed, we created humans in the best form.
But we will reduce them to the lowest of the low 'in Hell'
Except those who believe and do good-they will have a never-ending reward.
Now, what makes you deny the 'Final' Judgement?
Is Allah not the most just of all judges?"

Finding the fruits of Jannah

"Here we are," said Grandma as they arrived at the local supermarket. "Here, take this basket and pick out the fruits you would like for our drink, maybe you will see some of the fruits of Jannah." smiled Grandma.

"Okay," Aisha said excitedly, as she took the basket and started to look around the shelves packed with all the different types of fruits and colours. "Now let me try and remember what they could be?" she said quietly to herself. After searching for a while, Aisha saw what she wanted and put them in the basket. Grandma was in the next aisle and had just finished picking up some vegetables.

"Maa, maa!" called Aisha after she had finished picking out her fruits. "I can't carry this basket, it's too heavy!"

Grandma quickly went to Aisha and took her basket.

"Wow Aisha, good job with picking all these fruits! Let's go and pay for this now."

Grandma first took out the vegetables and then the fruits and placed them on the counter.

"These are some interesting fruits you have chosen, Aisha. Why did you choose these?"

"It's the fruits from the Qur'an, Maa. I remembered them," replied Aisha. She pointed to each fruit and said their names out in Arabic, this is Talh-bananas, Teen-figs, Ruman-pomegranate, Thamar-dates those are my favourites" giggled Aisha, "I eat them every day. But there's one fruit missing Maa, I couldn't find it," said Aisha.

Grandma knew exactly what was missing and quickly went to get a jar of olives. "Here you go Aisha, Zaytoon. "Oh yeah! Like the name of the Surah!" said Aisha excitedly.

"I don't think we can add these into the drink," laughed Grandma pointing to the jar of zaytoon," But let's see what we can make with all these other lovely fruits,"

Can you guess what fruit Zaytoon is?

Allah blesses the lands with fruits

The sun was shining brightly, Ahmed and his friends were playing in the garden and Mum was preparing dinner. Grandma and Aisha were cutting up the fruit to make their drink.

"Since Hasan is here, let's make a nice cool date and banana milkshake, I'm sure the dates will remind him of Palestine." said, Grandma.

"Ooh, that sounds yummy!" said Aisha excitedly.

Grandad came to help too. He helped remove the seeds from the dates while Aisha peeled the bananas. Grandma gave the boys a large bowl with cut pomegranates so they could remove all the fruit seeds from their skin.

Dad helped make a colorful salad, with green lettuce, purple figs, red pomegranates, and tomatoes. He also put a bunch of red grapes and olives into separate bowls and set the table. The table was full of wonderful colors and dishes.

It was a beautiful, warm evening. Bilal's family and Hasan's parents came over and joined them for dinner.

"That was a beautiful dinner! Jazaka Allah Khair." said Hasan's mum.

Hasan's Dad took a piece of fig in one hand and an olive in the other, "These fruits remind me of Palestine, we could just pick them from our trees."

"Please, tell us about Palestine," said Grandma.

Hasan quickly jumped in, "Oh Maa, it is so beautiful there and so very special to us. It has the third holiest mosque in the world - Al Aqsa, the place where our Prophet Muhammad (SAW), led all the Prophets in prayer, and did the night journey called the Miraj. There are a lot of Prophets who have lived and are buried there, as well as some of the companions of the Prophet (RA). Sadly, the occupiers are making it very hard for us to pray there and even for the people to live freely. But, Alhumdulilah, the land is very blessed. We can hear the call of prayer five times a day, and the weather is so nice that we can grow a lot of fruits like the ones we have on this table." Everyone nodded in agreement.

"Masha'Allah the land sounds very beautiful," said Grandma, "But, it is very sad to hear what is happening over there. May Allah (SWT) grant peace and security to the people of Palestine soon, Ameen" Everyone replied with Ameen.

As everyone was chatting, Aisha walked over to Grandma and whispered something to her ear.

"Oh, thank you for reminding me!" Grandma quickly got up and went into the kitchen and brought out the tray of milkshakes. Aisha ran to help share them out.

"We were so busy talking, I completely forgot about the drinks that Aisha and I made today," said Grandma.

Grandma with a big smile, handed Hasan's dad a glass, "Here, try this," Hasan's Dad was the first to take a sip, "This is delicious Masha Allah! I can taste dates in it and bananas?"

Aisha smiled, "Yes, it is Thamar wa Talh, (date and banana)."

"Your Arabic is very good! Masha Allah." Hasan's dad was impressed "Alhumdulilah, we've been learning about the names of fruits from Jannah in madarasah," replied Aisha happily and started to read out all their names as mentioned in the Qur'an.

Can you remember the names of the fruits mentioned in the Qur'an?

What can we learn from the story?

Allah says in the Qur'an:

"Exalted is He who took his servant 'Muhammad' by night from the sacred mosque 'at Makkah' to the farthest mosque 'al-Masjid al-Aqsa' whose surroundings We have blessed, to show him of our signs. Indeed, He is the Hearing, the Seeing" (Surah Al-Israa 17:1)

Palestine is a blessed land, it is through the Greatness and Mercy of Allah (SWT), that many fruits and vegetables are grown so that we can enjoy some of the fruits found in Jannah while living here on earth. It is also where our Prophet Muhammad (SAW) was transported from Masjid Al-Haram to Masjid Al-Aqsa and ascended to the heavens on a miraculous night journey called Al-Isra' wal-Mi'raj. It is the third holiest Mosque in Islam after the Ka'aba, in Makkah, and the Masjid An Nabawi, in Madinah.

It is mentioned in the books of Hadith, that Abu Darda (RA) narrated, the Prophet (SAW) said, *"A prayer in Makkah (Ka'aba) is worth 100,000 times (reward), a prayer in my Masjid (Madinah) is worth 1,000 times and a prayer in Al-Aqsa is worth 500 times more reward than anywhere else". (Bayhaqi)*

Since time began, Allah sent Prophets and Messengers to its people to teach them about the Oneness of Allah and the message of Islam. The Prophets taught them to obey Allah and follow his commandments; like how to live, work, and respect one another.

Allah says in the Qur'an, 'those who follow Him will be successful'.

Over time, some people became disobedient, neglected the teachings, and started to follow their desires creating problems in the lands and making it hard for people to live in peace.

Today, Muslims are faced with many hardships and difficulties.

May Allah keep the Muslims strong in their belief and have trust in Him, and Grant them peace and security under Islam. **Ameen.**

**Learning from the Qur'an
with Ahmed and Aisha**

The Sun or The Moon,
which is Greater?

The Sun or The Moon, which is Greater?

Aisha loves it when her grandparents, come over for a visit. They will play with her, take her out, and always take the time to answer her questions.

"Dada?" said Aisha as they were walking to the park one day.

"Yes?" smiled Grandad, knowing that Aisha would be asking one of her questions.

"The sun is so high up and we're down here. How does it give us so much light, and how does it make the day very hot when it's so small?"

"Aah, but the sun is not as small as you think it is, Aisha!" Grandad stopped walking and pointed to the bottom of the road. "Do you see that letter box at the end of the road? It doesn't look that big from here right now, but you know it's a lot bigger when it's closer. It is the same with the sun or anything that is far away. And, as for how the sun gives us light and heat, Allah (SWT) has made the sun from a big ball of fire and gas generating heat and light. And that is why it is so hot!"

Aisha's looked up at Grandad with her eyes and mouth opened wide. She looked like she was about to say something, but then looked down and shrugged her shoulders. She did not quite understand all the big words yet.

Grandad laughed, "Generate means to make, and the sun uses its energy to make heat and light." Grandad continued. "Do you remember when we went camping last summer and your dad lit a fire? Do you remember what happened when he rubbed the flint, the stone onto the metal piece of steel?

It produced fire, which is both light and heat. Or, have you ever seen your mum boil water in a pot? At first, the water warms up slowly, and after a few minutes, the water starts to bubble when it gets really hot!" Grandad started to shake his hands and his body around quite fast pretending to be the bubbles boiling in a pot. Granddad always made Aisha laugh.

"Aisha, take out your hands and put them together like this," Grandad showed her with his hands. "Now start to rub them together up and down, faster, and faster and faster. There! What did you feel Aisha?"

"My hands are getting quite warm Dada," said Aisha excitedly. "Exactly! Aisha, well done, you have made heat like the sun, now imagine there are a billion little hands like yours in the sun making heat." Grandad chuckled as they started to walk toward the park.

Is the sun greater than the moon?

Grandad was sitting on the bench reading his newspaper, while Aisha played in the sandpit with two of her friends from school. They used their bucket and spades to make a big castle and decorated it with objects that had fallen from the trees like leaves, acorns, and pinecones.

The day was very bright and all three girls were wearing their sunhats and shades.

"Look at the sun, it's so nice and bright, see how it glows in the sky," said Sarah standing tall, raising her arms into the air.

"But it's too hot," replied Lily. "The moon is so much cooler, and its so beautiful when its white light shines so brightly in the night."

Aisha heard her friends talking and started thinking to herself.

When it was time to go home, Aisha asked Grandad how the sun and moon know when to rise and set and which one was greater.

Grandad recited the fortieth verse of surah Yaseen.

"Bismillaahir – Rahmaanir - Raheem.

It is not allowed (possible) for the sun to reach the moon, nor does the night overtake the day. But each in an orbit is swimming."

"You see Aisha, Allah separated the day and night Himself. so, we can use the day for work, school, and play," Grandad smiled at Aisha. "And the night is for rest. These are the blessings and signs from Allah."

As they carried on walking home, Grandad continued, "Do you remember the story of the Prophet Ibrahim (AS)? Before he knew who Allah (SWT) was, he looked up at the sky at night and saw the stars, and said the stars were his Lord. But when the star set in the morning, he said they could not be his Lord because they went away.

Then on the next day, he saw the moon rising and said that the moon was his Lord, but when the moon set in the morning, he said it could not be his Lord as it also went away. And then in the morning, when Ibrahim saw the sun rising, he said that the sun was his Lord because it was greater than both the stars and the moon. But when the sun had set, what do you think Ibrahim (AS) thought to himself?"

"That the sun is not Allah. He said that he would pray to Allah who made everything in the sky and the world," replied Aisha confidently.

"Masha Allah Aisha, you remember the story!" With a big smile, Grandad took Aisha's hand and they both headed home.

Surah As-Shams – The sun

After tea and getting some rest. Grandad and Aisha got ready to go to the masjid as it was time for her madrassah class.

"Assalamu Alaikum wa Rahmutalahi wa Barakatahu," greeted Ustadha Maryam. Ustadha Maryam was Bilal's mother and Aisha's Qur'an teacher.

"Wa Alaikum Salaam wa Rahmutalahi wa Barakatahu." Replied the class.

"I hope everyone had a wonderful day today insha'Allah. Remember to always pray to Allah and thank him for all the things he has given you." Ustadha Maryam said. "So, what are we grateful for today?"

Aisha put her hands up first. "Ustadha, Allah gave us the sun. It was so warm and sunny today, Alhamdulillah, I'm grateful to Allah because I wouldn't have been able to play in the park with my friends if it was dark and cold."

"Masha Allah Aisha, that is very nice," replied Ustadha Maryam.

"And I am grateful to Allah, because after madrasah," Aisha continued, "I can go home and rest because I'm tired after playing so much in the park." Aisha slumped back on the chair. "Phew!"

Everyone in the class laughed.

"Well Aisha, since you are talking about the sun, Alhumdulilah, you have introduced the class to the new surah that we will be learning today- Surah As-Shams! As-Shams means The Sun. Let's begin the first five verses of As-Shams, Bismillah." And so, Ustadha Maryam began to recite: -

*"Aoodhu billahi mina-shaytaanir-rajeem,
Bismillahir Rahmanir-Raheem*

*By the sun and its brightness,
And by the moon when it follows it,
And by the day when it displays it,
And by the night when it covers it,
And by the sky and He who constructed it."*

What can we learn from the story?

In Surah As-Shams, Allah (SWT) swears by the sun and the moon and orders them to rise and set at their fixed times. They worship Allah and obey His orders. We are grateful to Allah (SWT) for the day and night so that we can work, play, rest, and worship Allah. Alhumdulilah, the five daily prayers can help us organise our days. May we all have lots of success in our lives while obeying Allah. **Ameen.**

Learning from the Qur'an with Ahmed and Aisha

Time

Time

It was the school holidays, and Ahmed and Aisha got up unusually early. They were excited because they were going to the airport with their Dad to collect their cousin Sulaiman. He was coming from Madinah, in Saudi Arabia to stay with them for a few days.

Sulaiman had just completed his Islamic Degree at Madinah University and was coming to work at an Islamic college in the city to teach Arabic and Islamic studies.

"Assalamu Alaikum, Uncle," Sulaiman called waving his hands excitedly. He was pushing a trolley with a large suitcase and a backpack.

"Wa Alaikum Salaam, Sulaiman! Allahumma Baarik, look at you!" Dad gave Sulaiman a big hug. "You're looking well, Alhumdulilah."

Sulaiman was the son of Ahmed and Aisha's Aunty-their Dad's sister. Their family had been living in Saudi Arabia since Sulaiman was five years old.

"Alhumdulilah, I am well, Mum and Dad are fine too. They sent their salaam and were very thankful that you're having me stay with you!"

"Wa Alaikum Salaam, we are very happy to have you staying with us. Insha'Allah we will call your parents when we get home," Dad replied.

Sulaiman then looked at Ahmed and Aisha with a big smile. "Assalamu Alaikum, Ahmed and Aisha. Wow, you've grown so big! Ahmed, you're almost as tall as me."

Ahmed was eight years old and was just over half the size of Sulaiman in height, but it made him happy to know that he was growing tall.

"Wa Alaikum Salaam," said Ahmed. "It is so nice to see you again!"

"Alhumdulilah, it is nice to see you all again too." Ahmed and Aisha looked at each other and smiled, they were going to enjoy having Sulaiman over to stay.

Ahmed was the first to open the door of the house and greet everyone with salaams and tell them that his cousin Sulaiman had arrived. Grandad with Grandma got up quickly to come to greet their grandson Sulaiman.

"Assalamu Alaikum Sulaiman!"

"Wa Alaikum Salaam Dada," Sulaiman kissed his Grandad's forehead and gave him a big hug. He then went to his Grandma and did the same.

"It's so nice to see you after two years!"

"Yes! It has been too long, Alhumdulilah you are here." Grandad patted Sulaiman on his back.

Sulaiman followed Grandma and Granddad into the house and was greeted by Ahmed's mum.

"Asslamu Alaikum Sulaiman, how are you?"

"Wa Alaikum Salaam Aunty, Alhumdulillah, I am well," Sulaiman greeted his Aunt by placing his right hand over his chest out of respect. "Thank you for hosting me Aunty, I hope I will not be a burden to you all."

"Not at all! It is our pleasure. Please come in," Everyone followed Mum into the living room. Sulaiman told them about his flight, his studies, and his life in Saudi Arabia.

"Alhamdulillah, I was able to memorise the Qur'an and gain an ijaza from my teacher so I can teach it now too. I learnt a lot from him, he is very well versed in hadith as well as the Arabic language. Alhumdulilah, I can understand the Qur'an properly and can explain it to others too, Insha'Allah."

"Masha Allah, we are all very proud of you! May Allah grant you lots of success, Ameen!" Said Grandad proudly.

Sulaiman turned to face Ahmed, "Ahmed, tomorrow, how about we walk around the city, and visit the college I will be joining Insha'Allah."

Ahmed smiled, "Thank you Sulaiman, can my best friend Bilal come too? He lives next door," said Ahmed.

"Of course!" said Sulaiman. "That sounds like a good plan."

Ahmed learns a new prayer

Ahmed woke up from his sleep, he heard some faint voices coming from the living room, but it was still dark outside. The hallway light was shining through the gap from his door. He quickly got out of bed and opened the door wider to hear the recitation of the Quran. Dad and Sulaiman were praying salaah. Ahmed rushed to do wudu (ablution) to join them. When Ahmed arrived downstairs, his dad and Sulaiman had finished praying. "Baba, what were you praying? I thought we prayed our Isha and my alarm for Fajr did not go off yet. What is this prayer?" asked Ahmed.

"Ahmed, come here," Ahmed's Dad smiled seeing Ahmed come down in the middle of the night to join them. Ahmed went to sit between his Dad and Sulaiman.

"We were praying the night prayer called Tahajjud. It's a nafl (voluntary). It is usually prayed anytime after Isha salaah and before the time of Fajr.

"Baba, have you been up since Isha salaah?" asked Ahmed.

"No! Ahmed," Dad smiled, "But, it is recommended to pray after taking some rest, and this is prayed in rakats of two, up to eight. Come let us pray two more rakats and finish off with the Witr salaah."

They got up and prayed their salaah, and then waited for the time of Fajr. Dad called the athan and they all prayed two rakats sunnah by themselves and then Sulaiman led the jamaah for the Fajr salaah.

Ahmed felt very tired; he was not used to waking up so early. He got up to go back to sleep and his cousin Sulaiman got out the Qur'an and began to recite it. Ahmed smiled and said his salaams.

Islam provides happiness

In the morning, Bilal came over when Ahmed and his family were having breakfast. "Alhumdulilah, I came just in time for a second breakfast," said Bilal cheerfully. Everyone laughed and welcomed him.

"I have to check if my room will be ready on time as I will be staying in the accommodations provided by the college." said, Sulaiman.

Ahmed looked a bit surprised and sad. He knew Sulaiman was only staying with them for a few days, but he enjoyed having him around and would miss him.

"Don't worry Ahmed," Sulaiman could see the change in Ahmed's face. "I'll be able to visit here at the weekends and you're most welcome to visit me too."

Ahmed smiled and gave a small nod.

"Come on, we need to go to the station and catch the train otherwise we will miss it!" said Sulaiman.

"Everyone is so busy on their mobile phones. Hardly anyone is talking or reading," said Sulaiman, observing the people on the train.

Ahmed and Bilal looked at each other and giggled. They didn't usually travel by train, and it was an exciting new experience for them.

Sulaiman was a very cheerful and kind person. He spoke well with a clear voice and greeted people with a nod and smile. They spent their journey laughing and discussing school, football, and food.

Sulaiman and the boys arrived at their final station. They walked towards the escalator and heard music being played by buskers, some people threw money into their boxes, while others walked past. As they came out of the station, they were shocked and saddened by the number of homeless people they saw in their sleeping bags or sitting on the streets with cardboard signs asking for some change. It was a sight that no one should see or go through.

Sulaiman shook his head with sadness, "Subhan' Allah, may Allah help these people."

"Ameen." All three of them said.

Ahmed and Bilal were feeling very sad and asked if they could help.

"Masha'Allah, it's wonderful that you're already so caring. Insha'Allah we can help them by buying some food."

Ahmed and Bilal liked the idea, they all went to a nearby supermarket and bought what they could. They handed the food to whomever they saw was in need. But it made them sad to know that this wasn't enough to make their lives better.

Omer Bin Al Khattab, the second caliph of Islam and a close companion of the Prophet Muhammad (SAW) made it a responsibility for himself, as a leader, to go to all the streets of Madinah and search for any person in need. It was the duty of the caliphs to provide for those who are in need with the basics of food, clothing and shelter. It's very sad to see that today countries that have lots of wealth, and have access to the best technology, are still unable to help the poor people.

As they were walking across the city, they were amazed by the old buildings mixed in with the new, tall glass buildings. They went passed by all sorts of shops, cafes, and restaurants. The streets were very busy and Ahmed and Bilal kept very close to Sulaiman as they didn't want to get lost in the crowds. They walked until they arrived at the college, which was called Al Maarifa (The Knowledge).

"Alhumdulilah, we are here. Bismillah!" said Sulaiman, as he and the boys walked into the building. They were welcomed into a warm and inviting large entrance hall. There were plants and picture frames with Quranic ayahs decorating the entrance wall. There was also the sound of the Quran being played gently in the background. The atmosphere was very calm. Sulaiman walked up to the receptionist, who was sitting behind a desk, and asked to see the Mudeer (headteacher). A few minutes later the Mudeer arrived.

"Assalamu Alaikum Sulaiman," a tall, older man with a warm smile, came to greet him. "Alhamdulillah, I am so happy to see you. Welcome!

"Thank you, Sheikh, I am very happy to be here!" They shook hands and then Sulaiman introduced the Mudeer to both Ahmed and Bilal. The Mudeer was happy to see them, and they were all invited to his office for a chat and some lunch. The Mudeer and Sulaiman discussed Madinah University and the course Sulaiman will be teaching at Al Maarifa. The Mudeer was very happy having Sulaiman being part of his team.

The athan for Dhuhr salaah was called just as they were finishing their lunch. The Mudeer led them to the wudu area and then the large prayer hall, where they saw lots of other teachers and students. One of the teachers led the prayer in jamaa and after its completion, people started greeting each other with salaam and started chatting. Ahmed loved the warm atmosphere of the prayer hall, it felt like home.

Sulaiman, Ahmed, and Bilal gave their salaams, and headed out of the building back to the busy streets of the city.

"Alhumdulilah," Sulaiman smiled. "Did you like the college?"

"Yes, said Ahmed excitedly. "It's so lovely! You're very lucky to be working there every day."

"Yes, I am looking forward to it," said Sulaiman with a big smile.

Sulaiman kept Ahmed and Bilal close to him as they walked on the busy streets. On the way, they stopped at a big stationary shop where Sulaiman bought some stationary for his new classroom and office. Ahmed and Bilal bought themselves a couple of pens and some fun- shaped erasers, like fruits and cars for their siblings.

It was late afternoon, and the trains had become very busy at the station with everyone rushing to grab a seat. Sulaiman and the boys stood at the end of a carriage, with Ahmed and Bilal holding onto him to stop themselves from falling. Everyone was minding their own business. They looked down at the floor, or their phones, or had closed their eyes with headphones in their ears. But people hardly smiled. It was a very different atmosphere and feeling from what they had experienced at the college.

After reaching home, the boys got themselves washed up and ready to join the rest of the family with Bilal's family, for dinner. Bilal and Ahmed told them about their journey on the train and how everyone was busy, rushing around. They also spoke about how they felt when they saw the homeless people on the streets, and the nicest feeling they had when meeting with the Mudeer and everyone at the college.

"Don't forget the man who was drooling while sleeping on the train," giggled Bilal.

"Well, you certainly saw a lot!" laughed Ahmed's Dad,

"Yes, but the best time we had was at the college," said Bilal, "Yes! we all prayed Dhuhr together and the atmosphere was so peaceful, Masha'Allah," added Ahmed.

Sulaiman smiled and said, "That reminds me of something Allah (SWT) says in the Quran in Surah Ar-Rad (13:28):

"In the remembrance of Allah, do hearts find rest."

"Alhumdulilah, that is very true! Wherever you went today, the conversations you had, giving charity, and enjoying good company at the college, you have filled your day and time with the remembrance of Allah. It's very important to keep good friends as they can remind us about good deeds and you'll feel at peace. We should try our best not to waste time but to please Allah; said Ahmed's Dad.

"Jazak Allah Khair Uncle, that is a very good reminder. This reminds me of a Surah which talks about time." said Sulaiman.

"Yes! You are right." said Grandad, "Sulaiman, Please recite to us Surah Al-Asr,"

Sulaiman nodded his head and started to recite Surah Al-Asr.

"A-oodhu billahi mina-shaytaanir-rajeem Bismillaahir-Rahmaanir-Raheem.

By Time, Man is indeed in loss, Except for those who have faith and do righteous deeds, And enjoin one another to follow the truth, and enjoin one another to patience."

What can we learn from the story?

Time is one of the greatest gifts Allah has given us. Those who use their time well in the remembrance of Allah, doing good actions, will be rewarded. Allah teaches us to do the actions that are commanded by Him so that we can come closer to Him; like to pray, give charity, and be with good friends. In the Surah al-Asr, Allah mentions that those people who keep themselves busy during the day in activities where there is no remembrance of Allah will be in a state of loss. May we never reach that state, but always spend our time, as much as we can in the remembrance of Allah. Ameen

It is narrated that our Prophet Muhammad (SAW) said about time: "There are two blessings which many people lose: (They are) health and free time for doing good" Bukhari

Questions to discuss:

Q. Why was the atmosphere between the Al Maarifa college and the journey on the train very different?

Q. What do you think will solve the problem of homelessness?